# HOCKEY'S
## —GREATEST—
# NICKNAMES

The Great One, Super Mario,
Sid the Kid, and More!

by
**THOM STORDEN**

CAPSTONE PRESS
a capstone imprint

Capstone Captivate is published by Capstone Press, an imprint of Capstone.
1710 Roe Crest Drive
North Mankato, Minnesota 56003
capstonepub.com

SPORTS ILLUSTRATED KIDS is a trademark of ABG-SI LLC. Used with permission.

Library of Congress Cataloging-in-Publication Data is available on the Library of Congress website.
ISBN: 9781663906953 (hardcover)
ISBN: 9781663920553 (paperback)
ISBN: 9781663906922 (ebook pdf)

Summary: Many of the greatest hockey players have earned funny, odd, or interesting nicknames during their careers. Read to find out the stories behind hockey's legendary nicknames.

Image Credits
Alamy: History and Art Collection, 13; Associated Press: Joe Giza, 16, Preston Stroup, 26; Getty Images: B Bennett, 24, Bruce Bennett, 18, David Cooper, 19, Focus On Sport, 17; Newscom: Sacramento Bee/ZUMAPRESS, 10; Shutterstock: Sashkin, Cover, Tiwat K, (doodle) Cover; Sports Illustrated: David E. Klutho, 6, 7, 8, Erick W. Rasco, 9, 14, Heinz Kluetmeier, 5, Hy Peskin, 21, 25, Manny Millan, 22, Robert Beck, 12, 28

Editorial Credits
Editor: Erika L. Shores; Designer: Terri Poburka; Media Researcher: Morgan Walters; Production Specialist: Laura Manthe

All internet sites appearing in back matter were available and accurate when this book was sent to press.

All records and statistics in this book are current through the 2020 season.

# TABLE OF CONTENTS

Words in **BOLD** are in the glossary.

# Nicknames of the Rink

## Puck Fact

Early hockey pucks were wood or stone. Today's pucks are rubber. Pucks are frozen before games so they won't bounce as much.

There's no game quite like hockey. Players with sticks battle in a rough game of keep-away with a small puck. They look for a chance to whack the puck into a net. All of this action happens while players wear ice skates.

Hockey players with nicknames are often the fastest skaters. There's Rocket, The Golden Jet, and The Roadrunner. Then there are nicknames for tough players, such as The Hammer and Knuckles. Other nicknames honor **legends**, such as The Great One. In a game of **slap shots**, saves, and power-play goals, hockey nicknames are sure to be fun.

Wayne Gretzky showing his skills on the ice in 1985.

*Sidney Crosby glides across the ice with a unique combination of speed and skill.*

**CHAPTER 1**

# Scorers

A hockey game doesn't usually have a lot of scoring. A single goal often decides who wins the game. When these goals happen, the players who score them are often cheered, admired, and nicknamed.

## SIDNEY CROSBY:
# Sid the Kid

In 2005 Sidney Crosby started in the National Hockey League (NHL). He was just 18. People called him the rhyming nickname of Sid the Kid because of his age. This standout player has led the Pittsburgh Penguins to three Stanley Cup wins.

Crosby has also been nicknamed The Next One. His skills as a player have been compared to NHL legend Wayne Gretzky. Gretzky was called The Great One. He played in the NHL from 1978 to 1999.

## JONATHAN TOEWS:
# Captain Serious

Jonathan Toews works and plays hard. His coaches noticed his serious style early in his career. Toews was made the captain of the Chicago Blackhawks at age 20. Young players rarely get the honor of being the team's leader.

Teammate Patrick Sharp says he gave Toews his nickname. Sharp first called Toews Mr. Serious. That name became Captain Serious after Toews became team captain.

Jonathan Toews takes control of the puck.

## MARK "Moose" MESSIER

At 6-foot-1 (185 centimeters) and 210 pounds (95 kilograms), Mark Messier was big and tough. His playing style was rough. He **checked** hard. He seemed to skate around looking for someone to run over. It's easy to see why Messier was nicknamed after a big, heavy, long-legged animal.

## BERNIE "Boom Boom" GEOFFRION

Bernie Geoffrion got his nickname at an early age. He would practice his powerful slap shot behind a local church. A reporter heard him practicing. He asked if Geoffrion would be OK with the nickname Boom Boom. Geoffrion agreed.

### Puck Fact

Mark Messier had a long NHL career with 26 seasons. He played 12 seasons with the Edmonton Oilers and won five Stanley Cups. He also won a Cup with the New York Rangers.

Mark "Moose" Messier in action during the NHL Winter Classic Alumni Game in 2012.

*Players from the New York Islanders surround Alex Ovechkin.*

## ALEX OVECHKIN:
# Alexander the Great

Alex Ovechkin led the Washington Capitals to the Stanley Cup in 2018. Ovechkin was also awarded the Conn Smythe Trophy that year as MVP of the playoffs.Ovechkin's great skills as a player earned him the nickname Alexander the Great.

# FRED "Cyclone" TAYLOR

One of hockey's first skating stars was Fred Taylor. Born in 1884 in Tara, Ontario, Canada, Taylor played for many teams including the Vancouver Millionaires. Taylor was fast on the ice. Because of his speedy skills, Taylor earned the nickname Cyclone. A cyclone is a fast, spinning column of air.

## BEST OF THE REST: Other Great Scorer Nicknames

Joe Sakic: **Mr. Clutch**

Peter "**The Great**" Forsberg

Pavel Datsyuk: **Magic Man**

Guy Lafleur: **Le Démon Blond**

Pavel Bure: **The Russian Rocket**

# CHAPTER 2

# Goalies

Dominik "The Dominator" Hašek stops the shot of Milan Michalek during an NHL playoff game.

The goalie is an easy player to spot. With all that extra padding, big mask, and giant gloves, this player stands out. It's no surprise that hockey goalies earn their fair share of nicknames.

## CURTIS JOSEPH: Cujo

It was easy to tell if goalie Curtis Joseph was in the net. His mask had a scary dog painted on it. Cujo was a popular horror novel and movie about a terrifying dog. Cujo combines the first two letters from Joseph's first and last name.

## DOMINIK HAŠEK: The Dominator

To dominate means to rule or control. And that's just the way Dominik Hašek played goalie. He controlled the net and kept **opponents** from scoring. Hašek got the nickname The Dominator early in his career. He won the Vezina Trophy for best NHL goaltender six times, all when he played for the Buffalo Sabres.

*Henrik "The King" Lundqvist focuses on the puck and makes a save.*

## HENRIK LUNDQVIST:
# The King

Henrik Ludqvist is from Sweden. When he played for the Swedish national team, the team's logo had a crown on the jersey. When he first joined the NHL in 2005, New York Rangers fans called him The King. Lundqvist won the 2011–12 Vezina Trophy. The award is given to the league's top goalie.

# "Tony O" ESPOSITO

The best a goalie can do is let nothing past him. Nothing, nada, zip, zero. With the number zero also known as the letter O, that led to Esposito's "Tony O" nickname. Tony O won the Vezina Award in 1969–70, 1971–72, and 1973–74. He played those seasons for the Chicago Blackhawks.

## COOL AS A CUCUMBER

Georges "Chicoutimi Cucumber" Vezina was a calm and cool goalie from Chicoutimi, Quebec, Canada. He starred for the Montreal Canadiens from 1910 to 1925. He passed away at age 39. The NHL named the award for best goalie each season the Vezina Trophy in his honor.

### TUUKKA RASK: **Tuukk**

Goalie Tuukka Rask's nickname isn't very different from his first name. Fans call out "TUUUUKK!" when Rask makes a great play. And Rask has made many great saves for the Boston Bruins since joining the NHL in 2007.

### GARY **"Bones"** BROMLEY

Gary Bromley was just 150 pounds (68 kg) during his time as an NHL goaltender. His skinny build earned him the nickname Bones. Bromley stood out in the net for another reason. When he played for the Vancouver Canucks, his goalie mask had a skull painted on it. It was the perfect mask for a player nicknamed Bones.

*Goalie Tuukka Rask (40) in the middle of the action during the NHL playoffs.*

## FRANK BRIMSEK:
# Mr. Zero

Frank Brimsek had two amazing streaks in the 1938–39 season. Mr. Zero allowed zero goals for 231 minutes and 54 seconds of play. His second streak was 220 minutes and 24 seconds. He won that season's Vezina Trophy and helped the Boston Bruins win the Stanley Cup.

## STEVE "The Puck Goes Inski" BUZINSKI

Steve Buzinski was the goalie who allowed Maurice "Rocket" Richard's first-ever goal in 1942. Richard became one of the best hockey players of all time. His score on Buzinski was the first of many goals. It was also just one of many goals let in by "The Puck Goes Inski" Buzinski. Buzinski played only one NHL season.

### Puck Fact
Tuukka Rask won the Vezina Trophy for the 2013–14 season.

## BEST OF THE REST: Other Great Goalie Nicknames

Walter "Turk" Broda

Felix "The Cat" Potvin

Eddie "The Eagle" Belfour

Andre "Red Light" Racicot

Lorne "Gump" Worsley

Jim Carey: Net Detective

Nikolai Khabibulin: The Bulin Wall

# CHAPTER 3

# Enforcers

Chris "Knuckles" Nilan (center) shoves Larry Murphy to the ice during a 1986 game.

Hockey has players who aren't afraid of playing rough. These players check opponents into the boards. They won't back down against an opponent. These tough players are often called **enforcers**. They also have earned a few other nicknames.

## CHRIS "Knuckles" NILAN

Tripping. Holding. High-sticking. Fighting. These are all names of hockey fouls. When hockey players break the rules, they get sent to the **penalty** box. One player who spent plenty of time there was Chris "Knuckles" Nilan. No player has racked up more penalty minutes in the long history of the Montreal Canadiens.

### Puck Fact

Knuckles Nilan was a member of the Montreal Canadiens Stanley Cup–winning team in 1986.

## DAVE "The Hammer" SCHULTZ

Dave Schultz was a member of back-to-back Stanley Cup winners in the mid-1970s. The Hammer was part of a Philadelphia Flyers team that played a very physical style of hockey. But not all rough behavior in hockey is allowed. There are penalties for breaking the rules. The Hammer holds the **record** for most penalty minutes ever in one season. He sat in the penalty box for 472 minutes in 1974–75. That's nearly eight hours!

*Dave "The Hammer" Schultz goes for the puck during a 1975 game.*

Wayne Gretzky (left) and Dave Semenko (second from left) celebrate a win with teammates in 1982.

**Puck Fact**

Stu Grimson published a book in 2019. It was called *The Grim Reaper: The Life and Career of a Reluctant Warrior.*

# STU "The Grim Reaper" GRIMSON

In 729 pro games, Stu Grimson scored just 17 goals. So how did he last 14 seasons in the NHL? Mainly, by fighting for it. The Grim Reaper was a play on Grimson's last name and a nickname for death. His tough style of play fit this dark nickname.

## DAVE SEMENKO: Cementhead

Many players rose to fame playing with Wayne Gretzky. Dave Semenko skated for the Edmonton Oilers in the 1980s. Semenko always had Gretzky's back. He would rough up any opponent who tried to get tough with Gretzky. Some called him Gretzky's on-ice bodyguard. Some just called him Cementhead.

## LARRY "Big Bird" ROBINSON

Sesame Street first became popular in the 1970s. One Sesame Street character is a tall, yellow, fluffy-haired figure named Big Bird. Oddly, that's how Larry Robinson sort of looked. Or at least Robinson's teammates thought so. They nicknamed their big, tough 6-foot-4 (193 cm) teammate after the character.

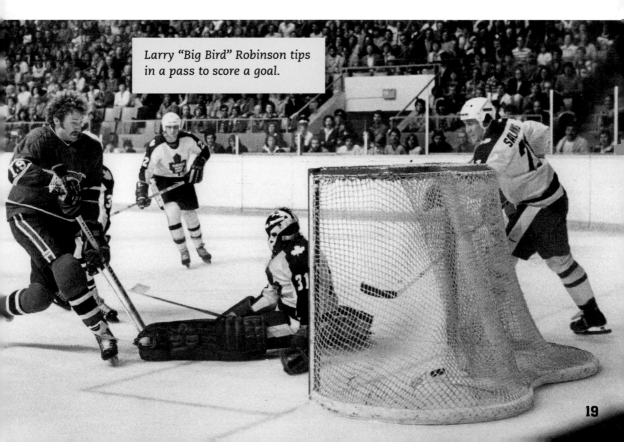

*Larry "Big Bird" Robinson tips in a pass to score a goal.*

## DAVE "Tiger" WILLIAMS

At age 5, Dave Williams was nicknamed by his hockey coach. That's because even at an early age, "Tiger" Williams was ready to pounce on opponents. Williams grew up to be a key part of five different NHL teams. He stood out for his goal-scoring as well as his toughness.

## GEORGE "Punch" IMLACH

George Imlach earned his fame as the coach of the Toronto Maple Leafs. But when he was younger, he was once knocked out while playing hockey. When he woke up, he was confused. He took a swing at the trainer who was trying to help him. That's how Imlach got the nickname Punch.

## "Terrible Ted" LINDSAY

On the ice, Ted Lindsay was rough and tough. His nickname Terrible Ted made sense. Off the ice, though, Lindsay helped hockey players earn better pay and **contracts**. Terrible Ted made the NHL better for his teammates and future players.

## THE PRODUCTION LINE

Ted Lindsay was a part of many great Detroit Red Wings teams between 1944 and 1957. The Red Wings best players from that time were known as The Production Line. That nickname was also due to Detroit being home to many car factories and their production lines.

*"Terrible" Ted Lindsay (left) stretching for the puck against the Montreal Canadiens in 1954.*

## BEST OF THE REST: Other Great Enforcer Nicknames

Francis Michael "**King**" Clancy

Wendel Clark: **Captain Crunch**

Frank "**Seldom**" Beaton

Johan Franzen: **The Mule**

# CHAPTER 4

# Hall of Famers

The Great One. Mr. Hockey. Super Mario. Even if one didn't know to whom those nicknames belonged, it'd be a good guess they were outstanding players. These nicknamed players aren't just amazing, though. They all belong to the NHL Hall of Fame.

*Wayne Gretzky takes a shot against the Montreal Canadiens.*

## WAYNE GRETZKY:
# The Great One

The owner of most major individual records in pro hockey history: Wayne Gretzky. The winner of four Stanley Cups: Wayne Gretzky. The greatest hockey player ever, according to most: Wayne Gretzky. It's no wonder Wayne Gretzky is known as The Great One.

## MARIO LEMIEUX: Super Mario

Mario Lemieux had 10 seasons where his goals and **assists** totaled 100 points or more. He was the NHL's top scorer six times. He won two Stanley Cups with the Pittsburgh Penguins. His Super Mario nickname came from his super skills and the popular Mario Bros. video game.

## A GREAT NICKNAME

Before he was even a teenager, Wayne Gretzky was given the nickname The Great One by reporter John Herbert. Gretzky's brother, Brent, was called The Other One. Brent played briefly in the NHL.

> Willie O'Ree gets control of the puck and takes it out from behind the net.

## WILLIE O'REE: The Jackie Robinson of Hockey

Willie O'Ree was called up to play for the Boston Bruins in 1958. He was the NHL's first Black player. People called him The Jackie Robinson of Hockey. Eleven years earlier, Robinson had become the first Black player in Major League Baseball. O'Ree had to endure name calling and unfair treatment often in his career.

### Puck Fact

Willie O'Ree made the Boston Bruins even though he lost sight in his right eye from being hit by a puck. For a long time, O'Ree told no one—not even his parents.

# MAURICE "Rocket" RICHARD

Maurice Richard was given his nickname because he skated like a rocket across the ice. He was the first hockey player to reach 500 career goals. He won eight Stanley Cups. Five of those wins were consecutive with the Montreal Canadiens.

# HECTOR "Toe" BLAKE

Growing up, Hector Blake's little sister couldn't say his name. She called him Hec-toe, and the name stuck. Toe Blake skated for the Montreal Maroons and Canadiens. One year he led the league in goals created. But he may have been an even better coach. He managed the Canadiens for 13 seasons. They won eight Stanley Cups.

Maurice "Rocket" Richard goes in at full speed to score a goal in 1954.

*Gordie Howe played for the Detroit Red Wings for 25 seasons*

## Puck Fact

Grodie Howe played into his 50s. It was long enough to skate alongside his sons, Marty and Mark. For seven seasons, they were teammates on the Houston Aeros and the Hartford Whalers.

## GORDIE HOWE: **Mr. Hockey**

Before there was Gretzky, there was Gordie. Mr. Hockey held many of the goals, assists, and scoring records that Wayne Gretzky broke. Howe's career was long and bright. Gordie Howe appeared in the NHL All-Star game 23 times.

## BOBBY HULL: **The Golden Jet**

Bobby Hull was one speedy skater. Hull's slap shot was also high-speed. Those factors along with his blond hair earned him the nickname The Golden Jet. Hull played his best years with the Chicago Blackhawks.

### Puck Fact

Bobby Hull's brother, Dennis, was his teammate on the Chicago Blackhawks for eight seasons. Dennis's nickname was The Silver Jet.

## BRETT HULL:
## The Golden Brett

Brett Hull followed in the footsteps of his father, Bobby, to hockey fame. Brett was given the nickname The Golden Brett. It played off his father's nickname, The Golden Jet. Brett Hull won two Stanley Cups to his father's one.

## BEST OF THE REST:
## Other Hall of Fame Nicknames

Glen "**Slats**" Sather

Nicklas Lidstrom: "**The Perfect Human**"

Teemu Selanne: "**The Finnish Flash**"

"**Lucky**" Luc Robitaille

Howie Morentz: "**The Stratford Streak**"

# CHAPTER 5

# The Wild and Weird

Some of the best nicknames are the weirdest. In the sport of hockey, there have been plenty of crazy characters. Check out these stickhandlers' handles.

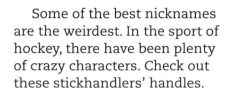

"Jumbo" Joe Thornton in control of the puck against the Anaheim Ducks.

## "Jumbo" JOE THORNTON:

Standing 6-foot-4 (193 cm) and weighing 220 pounds (100 kg), Joe Thornton is a big problem for opponents. Jumbo Joe was the large leader of the San Jose Sharks for most of his career before suiting up for the Toronto Maple Leafs in 2020–21.

## LOU "Leapin' Louie" FONTINATO

This tough-guy skater got his nickname from jumping up and down to complain about referees' calls. He was a defenseman for the New York Rangers and the Montreal Canadiens.

## YVAN COURNOYER: The Roadrunner

Yvan Cournoyer was just 5-foot-7 (170 cm), but he had blazing speed. A sportswriter nicknamed him The Roadrunner because of this. He helped the Montreal Canadiens to 10 Stanley Cups.

## VIC "Dit Clapper"

As a young child, Aubrey Victor Clapper wasn't able to say his own name. He called himself Dit. The name stuck. Dit Clapper played 20 seasons for the Boston Bruins. He was both a coach and a player for two of those seasons.

## KEN "Wolfman" MORROW

Ken Morrow got his nickname from the wolf-like beard he wore. New York Islanders fans from the 1980s loved his defensive game. Morrow won four Stanley Cups in his 10 seasons in the NHL.

### BEST OF THE REST:
### More Wild and Weird Nicknames

Garry "Iron Man" Unger

Al "Radar" Arbour

Derek "The Boogeyman" Boogaard

Igor "The Professor" Larionov

Fred "The Fog" Shero

# GLOSSARY

**assist** (uh-SIST)—a pass that leads to a score by a teammate

**check** (CHEK)—to block or stop

**contract** (KAHN-trakt)—a legal agreement between people stating the terms by which one will work for the other

**draft** (DRAFT)—an event in which athletes are picked to join sports organizations or teams

**enforcer** (in-FORS-ur)—a person who makes sure something happens; in hockey, an enforcer makes sure opponents are stopped from moving the puck down the ice

**legend** (LEJ-uhnd)—someone who is among the best in what they do

**opponent** (uh-POH-nuhnt)—a person or team who competes against another person or team

**penalty** (PEN-uhl-tee)—a punishment for breaking a rule in a game; a penalty shot is when a team plays shorthanded because one of their players is in the penalty box

**record** (REK-urd)—when something is done better than anyone has done it before

**slap shot** (SLAP SHOT)—the fastest and most forceful shot in the game; a player raises his or her stick and slaps the puck hard toward the goal, putting his or her full body power behind it

# READ MORE

**Keppeler, Eric.** *The Greatest Hockey Players of All Time.* New York: Gareth Stevens Publishing, 2020.

**Parker, Donald.** *Sidney Crosby.* Broomall, PA: Mason Crest, 2020.

**Walker, Jason M.** *Crosby vs. Ovechkin vs. McDavid vs. Gretzky.* New York: Rosen Central, 2020.

# INTERNET SITES

*Hockey Hall of Fame: Player Search*
hhof.com/html/search.shtml

*NHL Players*
nhl.com/player

*Sports Illustrated Kids: Hockey*
sikids.com/hockey

# INDEX